Achieving benefits from business change

Exploiting information systems

LONDON: HMSO

CCTA
The Government Centre for Information Systems

First published 1994

ISBN 011 330841 8

For further information regarding this publication
and other CCTA products please contact:

Library
CCTA
Rosebery Court
St Andrews Business Park
Norwich NR7 0HS

0603 704930

Contents

1 Introduction

Most organisations make substantial investments in information systems (IS) and information technology (IT) to support business objectives. The *costs* and *risks* of information systems are usually identified, tracked and managed throughout the life of a system. But the expected *benefits* are not always easy to identify and quantify. Many systems fail to deliver the benefits on which investment was justified.

This booklet will help business managers to obtain the benefits that their information systems are expected to achieve. It explains why benefits from IS/IT need to be actively managed. The booklet also provides guidelines on identifying benefits that support business objectives and managing the process of achieving the benefits that were the basis of the investment in IS/IT.

1.1 What are IS/IT benefits?

The benefits that can be achieved from IS/IT can be defined as:

the advantages or good produced with the assistance of computers and communications in support of business goals.

Whatever the benefit, the following conditions apply:

- they relate to business goals or objectives
- they may be *enabled* by specific information systems but require significant management action and effort to *realise* them
- they require measurement throughout the information systems lifecycle to determine whether or not they have been achieved.

1.2 A definition of benefits management

An information system cannot produce benefits without active management – the expected benefits can only be achieved by changing the way people work as a result of its implementation. To be managed, benefits must be visible. *Benefits management* is the identification of potential benefits, their planning and tracking, the assignment of responsibilities and authorities and their actual realisation.

But this is often overlooked, with the result that information systems may not deliver the specific benefits that were the basis for the investment, even if running the business without them is inconceivable.

1.3 Investment appraisal

Investment appraisal is a key aspect of sound financial management. It is the task of quantifying options for investment in IS/IT by showing the costs, risks and benefits. At the highest level, the IS Strategy Business Case will identify the benefits expected from the strategy. The strategy will be implemented by a series of programmes and projects, where the broad levels and types of benefits described are refined and quantified. *The benefits of each option will be expressed in cash terms in the investment appraisal, usually at project level. This is to allow a decision to be made as to which offers the greater overall benefits to the organisation, even though benefits may not ultimately be realised in cash terms.* Output from the investment appraisal is usually included as part of the final business case for an information system and provides the justification for the chosen system option.

Benefits management complements and overlaps investment appraisal, as shown in Figure 1.

While investment appraisal provides the justification for the investment, benefits management allows organisations to plan for and achieve the benefits. Costs and benefits cannot be viewed in isolation and organisations should plan the benefits management process and the overall investment appraisal together.

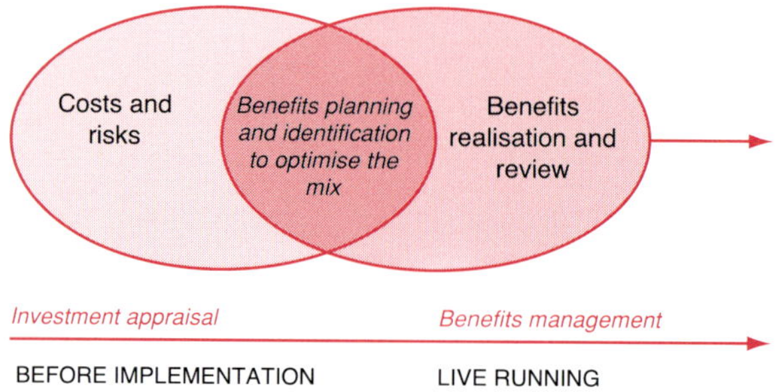

Figure 1 Relationship between investment appraisal and benefits management

Figure 2 shows how benefits relate to business drivers (requiring a business response) and the business case for investment in IS/IT. In order to achieve a desired outcome such as *improved service* it may be necessary to realise enabling benefits first, such as *properly trained staff*. The planned benefits are considered in the context of their estimated cost and risks to the organisation when preparing the business case for the investment.

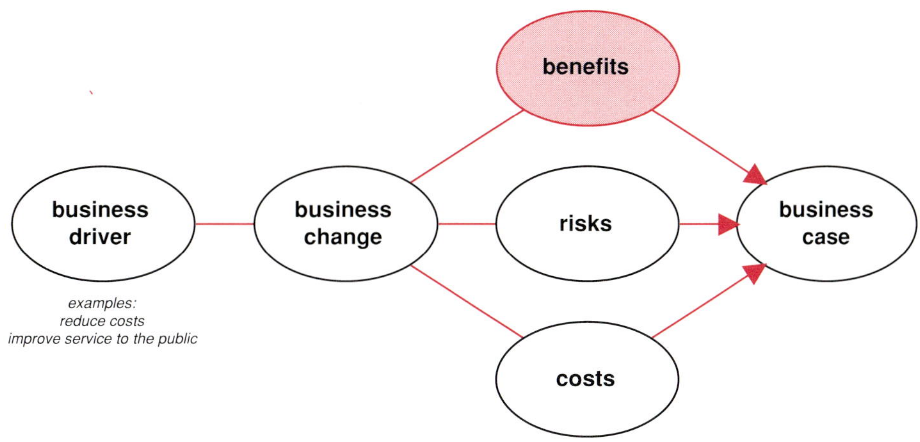

Figure 2 A benefits model in the context of the business case

1.4 What business managers need to know

In order to manage benefits effectively, business managers need to be able to answer the following questions:

- how do we identify potential benefits from this investment?
- how do we assess their relevance and priority to the organisation?
- how do we know if we are achieving them?
- what are the risks in achieving them?
- what are the risks in *not* achieving them?
- how do we identify and maximise unexpected benefits?
- how can we achieve more?

Considerations when addressing these questions are:

- collecting information to support the management of benefits costs money and consumes resource. The value of managing benefits will need to be agreed and demonstrated over time
- communicate the reasons for doing it, especially where benefits and costs cross organisational boundaries. Responsibilities must be clear and agreed
- the simple way to assess benefits is to compare actual and planned results
- measurement information is used to determine what actions need to be taken, if any. Any shortfall or over-achievement must be evaluated and action taken to continue to harvest maximum benefits from the investment.

2 Principles of benefits management

The scope of the process for managing the benefits from business change will vary according to the type and size of the programme or system under consideration and the organisation in which it is being implemented. There is however a set of fundamental principles that will apply to all IS/IT investments. These are summarised below and described in the following sections:

- there must be full investment in business change
- there may be many different types of benefit accruing to an organisation
- the scope of the benefits management exercise must be clear at the outset.

2.1 Investment in business change

Benefits arise from a full investment in business change, not just investment in an information system and the associated training. This change needs to be managed carefully and requires change management skills and resource. It is primarily the responsibility of business (user) management and requires commitment and support from management with the authority to resource it.

Examples of business change might be:

- process re-engineering
- job design
- organisational structure
- culture
- responsibilities
- staff numbers
- staff skills
- career structures
- staff remuneration
- physical environment
- the products and services offered to customers and their means of delivery.

2.2 Different types of benefit

Many different types of benefit may accrue to an organisation, enabled by the introduction of information systems. The importance attached to individual types of benefit will depend on what the organisation is trying to achieve. These are the **outcomes** that the organisation is seeking – not necessarily a saving in cash terms although it will often include this.

Benefits fall into three categories:

- those which can be quantified and valued (direct financial benefits)
- those which can be quantified, but are difficult or impossible to value (direct non financial benefits)
- those which can be identified but cannot easily be quantified (indirect benefits).

Direct financial and direct non financial benefits are relatively easy to identify and quantify. Direct financial benefits can be compared with each other in financial terms or to other ways of spending the money.

To assess properly the overall contribution of an information system, it is necessary to identify, measure and value (in terms of contribution to business objectives) direct non financial and indirect benefits.

Indirect benefits must be identified and prioritised, even though there may be no common currency between them. To do so requires that their contribution to business objectives is assessed. For a clear meaningful linkage to be made, objectives should be specific, measurable and achievable.

Benefits that are quantified have a better chance of being realised. But measuring and quantifying benefits will require resources.

2.3 Scope of the benefits management exercise

The scope of the benefits management exercise must be clear at the outset and must correspond to the scope of the investment appraisal for the proposed system. Benefits (and costs) which form the basis for investment may accrue across organisational boundaries, or possibly outside the organisation itself. Attribution of benefits must be clear and agreed. This may require business managers or organisations "signing up" to realising specific levels of benefit.

Specific responsibilities and authorities should be assigned to those charged with: planning tracking and realising benefits at all stages of the system lifecycle (from system development to the end of the system's life). A coherent framework for measuring and managing benefits as well as costs and risks provides consistency.

2.4 How are benefits managed?

The management policies in the IS strategy should describe what an organisation wishes to achieve from the benefits management process and how it will do so.

The process should not be over-complicated. It consists of a number of activities which feed each other and require review. Information gained at the start of the process is gradually refined as decisions are taken, so that business objectives are ultimately translated into actual measurable benefits. Figure 3 summarises the key activities.

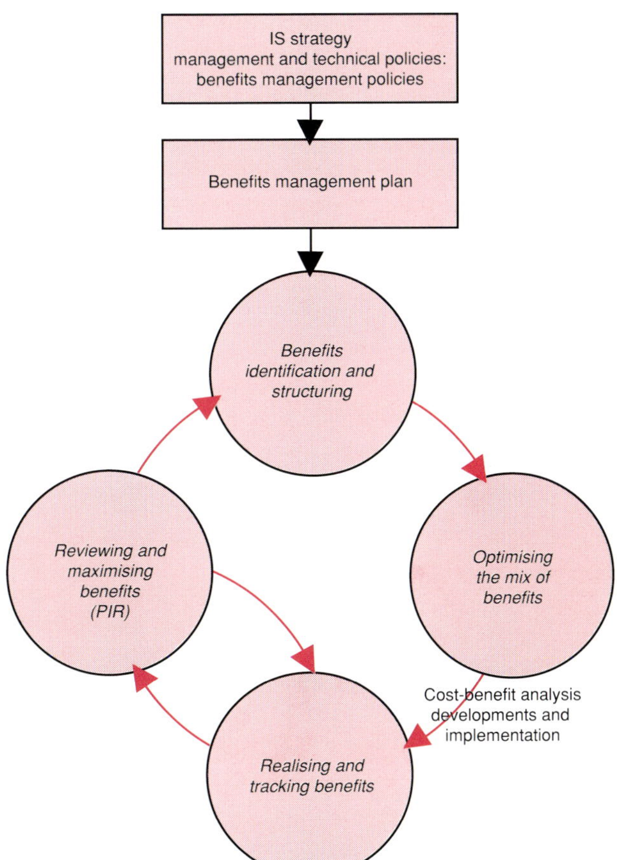

Figure 3 Benefits management activities

The activities are:

- **initial planning** for how the benefits will be managed. The IS strategy's management and technical policies should describe how the organisation wishes to manage and achieve benefits from any system. At individual programme or system level a more detailed plan will be required
- **benefits identification and structuring**. This involves identifying, for a system under consideration, what benefits can accrue to the organisation by investing in it. This involves assessing what they actually mean in business terms and understanding their dependencies and linkages
- **optimising the mix of benefits.** Choosing the business system option that delivers the best value to the organisation for the given set of business objectives and circumstances
- **realising and tracking benefits.** Having decided what benefits are expected, tracking their achievement needs to be planned; a measure and target assigned to them; and a data collection regime initiated
- **reviewing and maximising benefits**. Using the measures, seeing whether targets were reached and recommending action to achieve or maximise them and planning the next tranche (for programmes or larger systems) of benefits to be realised. This should continue throughout the life of the system.

The benefits cycle is shown in Figure 4 (opposite), in which the activities described above are related to stages in the cycle. Chapters 4-7 describe the process in detail.

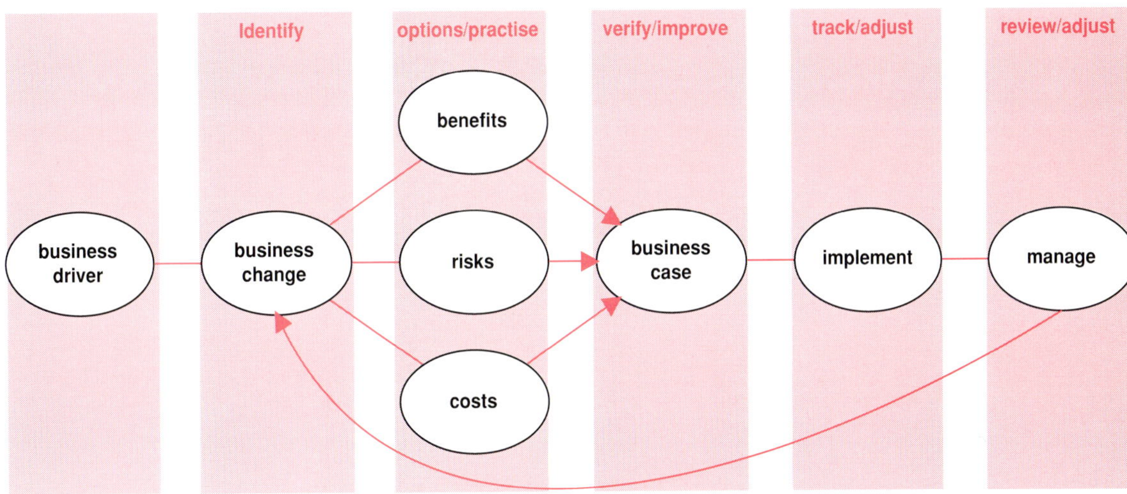

Figure 4 The benefits cycle

2.5 Programme management

Managing business change can bring particular problems in coordinating a number of related projects and achieving planned benefits. *Programme management* is an approach that provides a mechanism for achieving benefits from business change. The framework of programme management facilitates:

- the planning and execution of a portfolio of projects
- the delivery and review of associated benefits.

The *programme management executive team* is responsible for delivering the business change and helping to realise the associated benefits. This team includes key managers from the business area who have specific responsibility for benefits realisation.

2.6 Who is responsible for managing benefits?

The commitment to managing benefits must come from the owners of the IS strategy business case. While programme and project teams will be involved in projects delivering business change, *responsibility for managing and realising benefits rests with business users and managers.*

3 Planning

This chapter describes how the management of benefits is planned. It explains how benefits relate to business objectives, the organisation's priorities and its business environment and highlights the role of policies in managing benefits.

3.1 The planning process

Figure 5 shows the activities in the planning process from the perspective of managing benefits. It ensures that there is a focus on benefits, the *outcomes*, rather than just costs, the *inputs*.

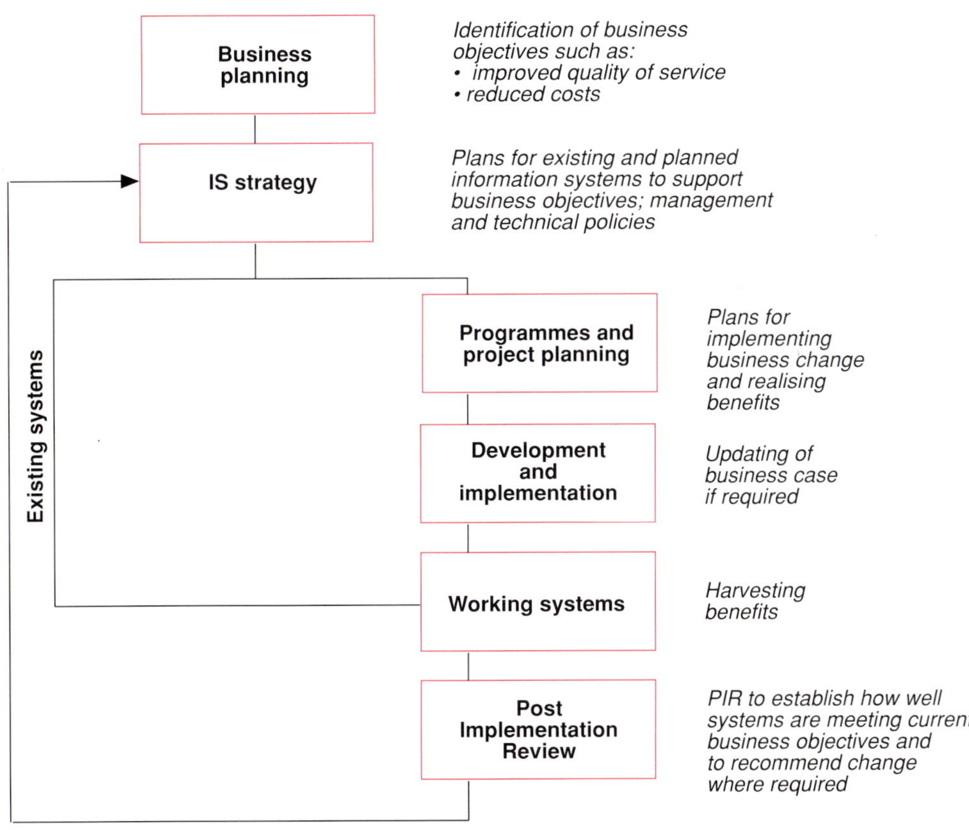

Figure 5 The IS/IT planning process

3.2 Policies for managing benefits

The organisation will need to have defined policies for managing benefits so that there is a consistent approach. The policies should form part of the *management and technical policies* in the IS strategy. The exact nature and detail of the policies will be determined by organisations individually, but each will have a common structure. The benefits management policy should contain as a minimum, the information below:

- why a policy on benefits management is needed (this will include senior management commitment to benefits management)
- who is responsible for ensuring the policy is adhered to
- how it is implemented (the mechanisms for making benefits management happen, identifying the benefits management activities and the sub processes described in Chapters 3 to 6 of this guide)
- who it affects and who will be affected, their responsibilities and authorities
- what the review requirements for the policy are (who reviews the high level policy and in what circumstances). This will usually be highlighted by the Post Implementation Review (PIRs) process.

3.3 Information for plans

The precise nature and content of plans for managing benefits will depend on an organisation's specific circumstances and will be driven by high level policies. The detail of the plans will vary depending on the project, but the minimum information required is:

- a clear description of the benefits management activities and their sequence
- the list of benefits and those assigned responsibility for delivering them
- the timescales of the exercise
- the resources required for the activities and when they are required.

3.4 The need for pragmatism

Each investment will require a different level of resource. Some examples of considerations which will decide the resource to be committed to the process of benefits management are given below:

- the management policies in the IS strategy – that is, the relative importance assigned to benefits management by the organisation
- the potential investment under consideration and the organisation in which it is being implemented (for example, less resource may be committed to benefits identification for a simple payroll system than to a system with the potential to change the way in which the organisation delivers its business objectives)
- the available resource within the organisation.

Existing, or 'legacy', systems pose particular problems because the business environment will have changed since the original IS/IT investment was made. The benefits required now will probably be very different from those originally planned. It is important to look at the changes that have taken place over a long period of time in order to determine what is worth monitoring now (see also section 7.6).

4 Identifying and structuring benefits

A business change may require an information system to help support business objectives. The benefits of the new business systems supported by IS/IT need to be made visible; they must be identified and described in order to be realised. This chapter outlines the different types of benefit that might be important to an organisation and provides some guidelines on how to define benefits and structure their sequence for a specific system. Figure 6 highlights the process of identifying and structuring benefits within the benefits cycle.

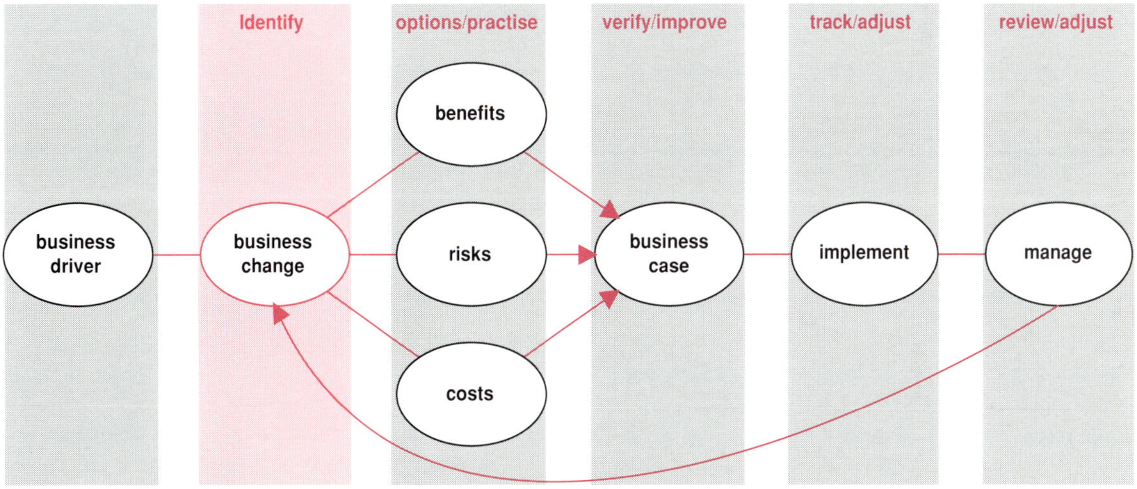

Figure 6 Identifying and structuring benefits

The activities required for defining benefits and structuring their sequence are:

- **identifying high level benefits** – these are the generic benefits (outcomes) that are important to the particular organisation directly related to the implementation of the information system. There will be a mix and this will depend on the organisation, what it is trying to achieve and the business objectives of the specific information system

- **top-down benefits identification** – this involves identification of all potential benefits, which will exist as a hierarchy, or structure (with dependencies) which implementation of the information system can enable.

Benefits identification is part of the Investment Appraisal activity. Like all elements of the business case, the detail on the amount and type of benefits will start with a broad estimate and will be refined as the programme or project proceeds, informed by other activities. It may be that benefits identified will be reviewed or changed entirely as the programme or project proceeds.

4.1 Objectives for business change

The potential information system will be part of the IS strategy portfolio of applications and may be implemented as part of a programme. A need for the system to enable business change will have been identified as part of the IS strategy study. Although the exact levels of benefit will not be known at this stage, broad orders of both benefit and cost should be available from the feasibility study report. The objectives for business change will be stated in terms of the benefits that the organisation wishes to gain from investment in the information system; these objectives will relate to the objectives in the IS strategy, which in turn support the objectives in the organisation's business strategy.

A useful classification for these benefits (which may be viewed as the outcomes required for the system) is:

- **Economy**. Concerned with obtaining the same goods or services more cheaply. The comparison may be made between suppliers, say, or over time. It is usually expressed in terms of savings
- **Efficiency**. A comparison of output with the input required to produce it. Unit cost is a measure of how much it costs to produce one unit of output and is another way of expressing efficiency
- **Effectiveness**. This is sometimes defined as "doing the right things well". It is the extent to which objectives have been achieved, expressed as the ratio of actual output to planned output.

This will enable organisations to identify broadly how they must realise benefits to produce favourable outcomes. For example, an information system may automate a clerical process and enable licence applications to be processed with 50% less staff resource. This will free up staff time. The way in which this is realised as a favourable outcome to the organisation will depend on the business objectives for the information system. It may be realised by reducing the number of staff (economy), allowing the same number of staff to process more applications (efficiency) or to process the same number of licence applications, cut timescales for doing so and offer a new service (effectiveness).

Realistically, a business change enabled by implementation of an information system may well offer a mix of all three classifications. These classifications can be useful for broadly defining information system objectives; however, they are of less use when considering exactly what business benefits are required of and enabled by information systems.

4.2 Identifying high level benefits

High level descriptions of benefits provide the starting point for relating IS/IT benefits to business objectives in the IS strategy. These descriptions are then refined at programme or system level.

This provides some structure for the benefits identification task and will assist in making subsequent benefits management activities (particularly, *Optimising the Mix*, described in Chapter 5), more meaningful and manageable by allowing benefits to be clearly understood in terms of contribution to business objectives. High level benefit headings help business managers to decide provisionally what business benefits the organisation wants from the information system.

The checklist below gives a number of high level benefits that may be applicable to organisations. It is neither prescriptive nor exhaustive. The important point is that organisations choose headings which are meaningful and helpful to the people who will be involved in the benefits management process and the decision to invest in the information system.

- **Mandatory (must do)**. Benefits which allow an organisation to fulfil policy objectives or satisfy legal requirements, where the organisation has no choice but to comply.
- **Quality of service.** Benefits to customers, such as quicker response to queries, providing more detailed, accurate information.
- **Internal management benefits**. Benefits which are internal to the organisation, such as improving the quality of decision making or management productivity.
- **Increased productivity.** Benefits which allow an organisation to do the same job with less resource, allowing reduction in cost, or to do more. This may also be termed **efficiency** or **cost avoidance** (where increased volumes can be handled with no increase in headcount).
- **More motivated workforce.** The benefits of a better motivated workforce may lead on to a number of other benefits – for example, flexibility or increased productivity.
- **Risk reduction.** For example, by offering flexibility – that is, not closing off courses of action, or providing new ones. In business or technical terms this allows an organisation to be prepared for the future.
- **Economy**. Reducing costs whilst maintaining quality. This may be termed **cost reduction**.
- **Revenue enhancement and acceleration.** Increasing revenue, or bringing in the same revenue quicker, or both).
- **Strategic fit.** Enabling the benefits of other systems to be realised.

Such high level benefits can then be mapped onto the classifications used for the business objectives of the information system. If the overriding business objective is to save money then economy will be of prime importance. If organisations expect a sharp increase in volumes of work, increased efficiency may provide the flexibility to take on this work. This mapping of high level benefits will give an indication of how benefits will be realised as outcomes but will not represent concrete decisions at this stage.

4.3 Linking high level benefits to business objectives

Direct financial benefits in support of business objectives are generally easier to justify than non financial benefits because they are of demonstrable value to the organisation. Example are freeing of accommodation or re-grading of work.

Non financial benefits at strategy level should be valid in the context of the business and this principle applies at all stages of IS/IT planning and management.

Business objectives should not be vague. Words like improve, maintain or reduce should refer to specific targets and when they should be achieved. They should be:

- unambiguous and results oriented
- measurable and verifiable
- relevant, achievable and encouraging higher performance
- driven by any higher level objectives.

Critical Success Factors (CSFs)

CSFs are the preconditions for business success and support business objectives. They are the areas that must perform satisfactorily, or well. CSFs are useful for linking potential benefits (financial or non-financial) to objectives.

4.4 Top-down benefits identification

The benefits identification task will identify the benefits that can accrue from the business change enabled by the implementation of the information system; it will also determine their structure.The benefits will fall into three categories. It is important that the category for each specific benefit is recognised as this will drive the measure applied to the benefit at a later stage. These are:

- those which can be quantified and valued (direct financial benefits)
- those which can be quantified, but are difficult or impossible to value (direct non financial benefits)

- those which can be identified but cannot easily be quantified (indirect benefits).

Figure 7 shows direct and non-direct benefits.

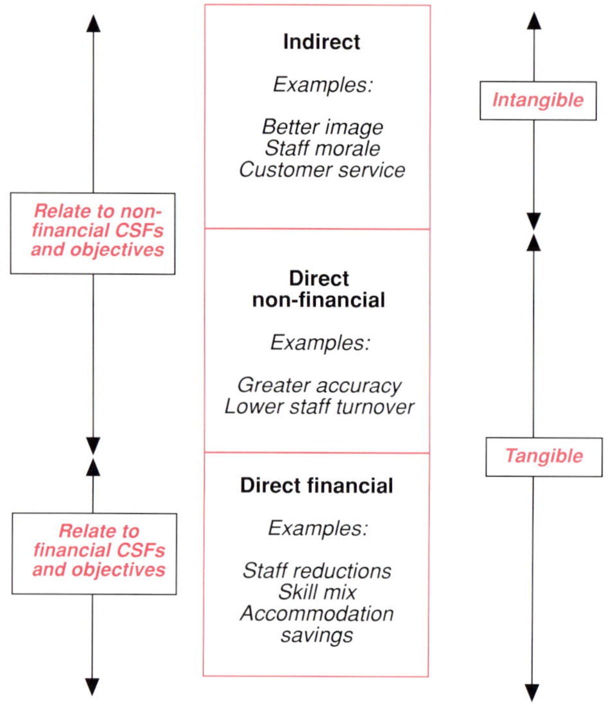

Figure 7 Examples of direct and non-direct benefits

Before the benefits identification task, it may be useful for those involved to ask - *what can the information system help us to do?* By relating these capabilities to the tasks currently carried out by the organisation (or business area where the information system is to be implemented) and to the business objectives of change for the business area, potential benefits may start to become more apparent.

Below is a basic checklist of things that the information system can *help* an organisation to do:

- improve decision making
- reduce labour costs
- automate physical processes
- identify problems and weaknesses
- transform business processes
- transform jobs
- identify new business opportunities
- help in the development of new products and services.

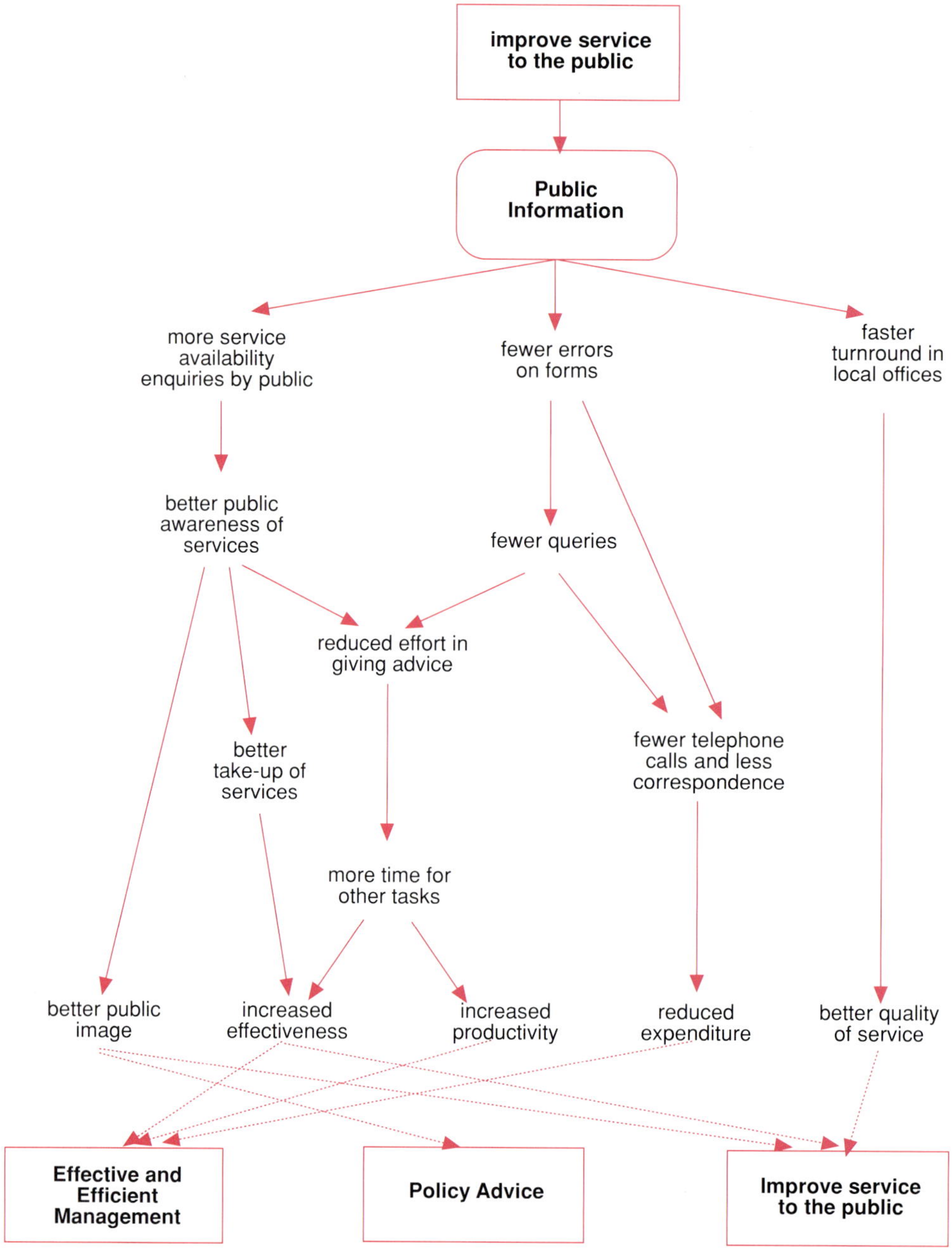

Figure 9 Benefits cascade

Two techniques which can be used separately or as complementary approaches to identify benefits are:

- **top- down analysis**. This approach focuses initially on business objectives to create a structure (or hierarchy) of benefits. An example of a top down analysis is a benefits "cascade", reproduced opposite (Figure 9)
- **system-led**. This can be used if the detailed benefits identification exercise is being conducted after system selection (or implementation), or as a review method after system specification to confirm previously identified benefits. The system features or functionality should be examined along with the business areas which the system is expected to affect. Each feature is then analysed to determine what benefits it can deliver (which will usually be at the bottom of the benefits structure). This approach should complement top down analysis.

  A summary of possible system features which offer potential benefits for which an organisation *may be prepared to pay* is given below:

  - *Speed*. The speed of the information system compared to manual methods
  - *Accuracy*. Avoiding the need for error correction
  - *Volume*. The ability of the information system to hold and manipulate higher volumes of data compared to manual holding and manipulation
  - *Security*. The importance and benefits produced by this feature vary widely depending on the organisation in which the information system is being implemented
  - *Automation*. This feature refers to automation which does more than simply speed up or increase the accuracy of a process. This may, for example, be knowledge based or expert systems where scarce or fallible expertise is replaced by computer analysis and a possible benefit could be the demonstrable equability of the information produced

- *Ease of use*. This feature of a system (for example, on line help screens) may enable benefits such as improved staff morale, or directly reduce the cost of training
- *Adaptability*. A system that is easily re-configured or adapted will offer an organisation flexibility to changing business requirements
- *Availability*. Information systems can make information available 24 hours per day, even outside normal working hours.

Most information systems will exhibit these features to a greater or lesser degree and the deciding factor will usually be the cost, so organisations must decide how much these attributes are worth to them. *Information systems do not deliver benefits in themselves. It is their use that delivers the benefits.*

The identification task will produce a number of potential benefits specific to the organisation; it will probably include benefits from the examples listed in Annex A.

4.5 Unexpected benefits

Introduction of information systems will change the way the organisation works and even the most rigorous benefits identification may not identify all benefits. The purpose of benefits identification is to identify as many potential benefits as possible. Chapter 6 gives details of how to identify unexpected benefits at the PIR stage.

4.6 Dis-benefits

A dis-benefit is *an unfavourable outcome*. In the same way that expected and unexpected benefits will accrue following introduction of an information system, dis-benefits will also occur and are identified as part of the benefits identification task. Organisations may wish to view and quantify (where possible) dis-benefits as costs or risks. Potential dis-benefits will occur for two reasons:

- those which are caused by badly executed design and implementation – for example, the processing time for claims forms could be increased following introduction of an information system (a dis-benefit) because users have not been properly trained

- those which are inherent in change, which no amount of planning or forethought can eliminate completely – for example, introduction of an information system may allow the transfer of responsibility for creation and maintenance of records from a central office to individual units. This may be an advantage to the organisation as a whole, saving the need for a separate office, but for the individual units taking on the new task, it is a dis-benefit.

The example above highlights the fact that a dis-benefit may be the result of a conscious decision by the organisation, where a dis-benefit allows a greater benefit to be realised.

Dis-benefits have to be managed in the same way as benefits; they must be identified, measured and tracked in order to minimise their impact. An example of this management could occur where an information system allows better information to be delivered. This may result in increased demand for the information (a dis-benefit to the business area that has to provide the information). The management action required is to ensure that the dis-benefit (the extra work required in the provisions of extra information) has a beneficial outcome – such as better, more informed decision making.

The effect of benefits management on benefits and dis-benefits is represented diagrammatically in Figure 10.

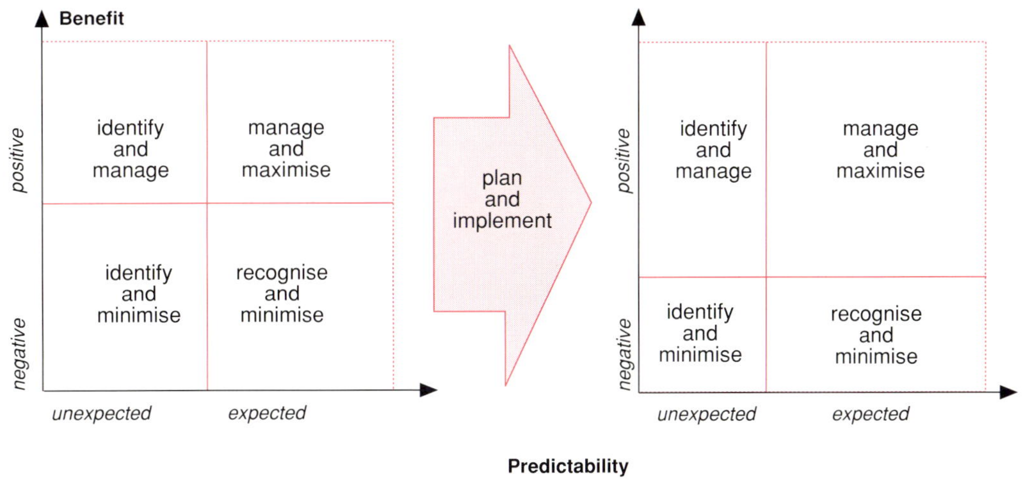

Figure 10 Managing benefits

4.7 Mechanisms for benefit identification

Whichever technique is used for benefits identification all or a combination of the following are likely to be used in the identification process:

- analysis of current activities and business objectives, CSFs
- consultation/interviews with the sponsors of the information system, business managers and users in the business area where the potential information system is to be implemented
- consultation with IS suppliers to identify broadly the business opportunities afforded by emerging technology
- consultation/interviews with business managers and users outside the business area where the potential information system is to be implemented to identify potential benefits and dis-benefits
- brainstorming to identify potential benefits the system could offer
- workshops.

4.8 Understanding the structure of benefits

Potential benefits that have been identified will not exist simply as a list. There will be links between *enabling benefits* and *benefits expressed* in the business case. It is important to recognise dependencies and linkages between benefits in order to determine where the achievement of a higher order benefit is dependent on the realisation of a lower order benefit. This approach enables the organisation to identify the management actions required to realise the benefits in the business case.

Benefits at the lowest end of the structure, for example reducing errors, speeding processing time, manipulating large data volumes quickly:

- will enable other benefits in the benefit structure
- will appear first (in terms of timescale)
- are most easily attributable directly to the introduction of the information system and the features it provides

- are realised with the fewest management actions
- are the most easily measurable and quantifiable
- are often not of significant value to the organisation *on their own* – that is, if they are not used to achieve higher order benefits, or outcomes.

The task of structuring benefits helps to clarify plans for realising benefits. Single enabling benefits can allow the realisation of a number of different desirable outcomes, as shown in Figure 8.

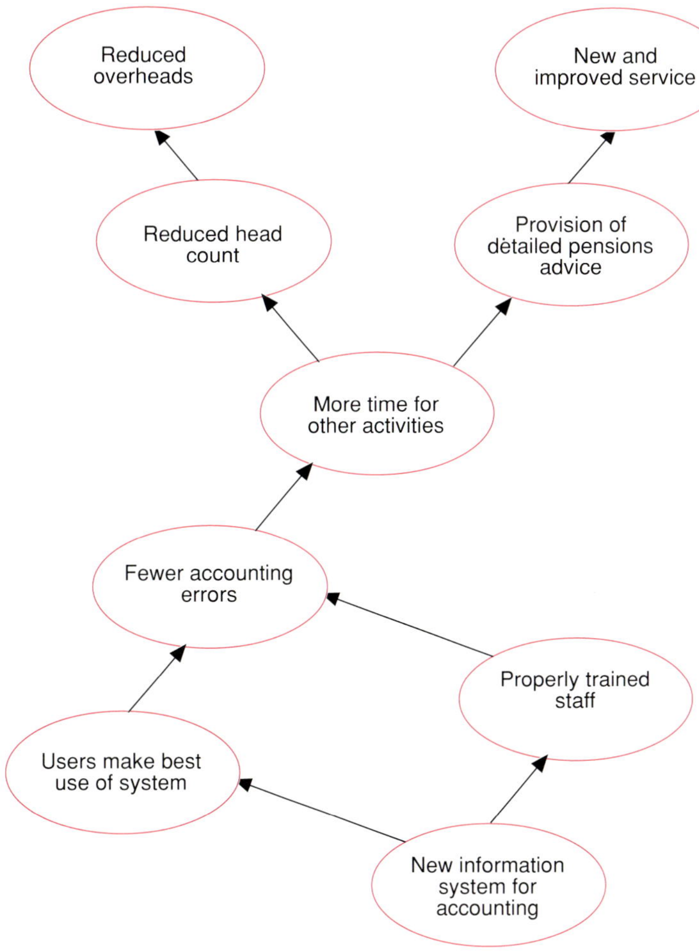

Figure 8 Benefits structure

5 Optimising the mix

No business change can provide everything that an organisation wants from it. Various options will have been considered in broad terms as part of the appraisal of the IS strategy. The detailed Cost Benefit Analysis will weigh up the full and detailed cost/benefit/risk equation at the stage when options are considered. Broad orders of cost will be available, however, before the detailed Cost Benefit Analysis. This chapter focuses on optimising the benefits delivered by different options.

There should now be firm options of business systems to be weighed up, each supporting the organisation in different ways and offering a different mix of benefits. This chapter explains how to choose the business system option that delivers the mix of benefits of most value to the organisation. Figure 11 highlights the stage of optimising the mix of benefits.

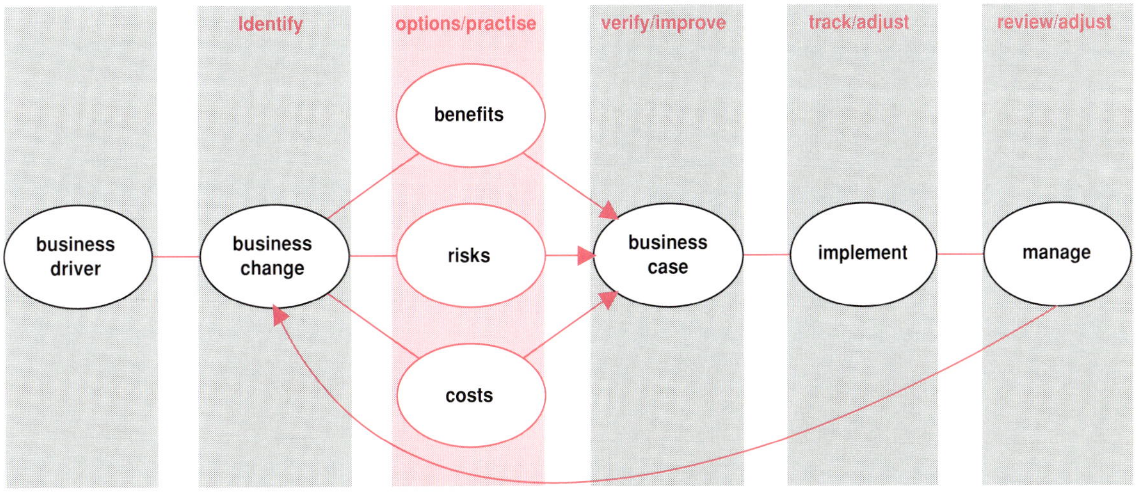

Figure 11 Optimising the mix of benefits

The tasks are:

- **option generation**. This task identifies a number of different ways of meeting business objectives including the do nothing option, or do minimum if something must be done, for example to comply with mandatory requirements. Each option will offer a different mix of benefits
- **choosing an option**. This task involves the ranking and scoring of options in order to arrive at the chosen option.

5.1 Option generation

Option generation involves firstly generating different business system options. Creating business system options involves examining the way in which prospective users of the system could perform tasks, the sequences in which they perform them and the outputs from those tasks. For larger systems, the boundaries between different business areas may be examined and challenged. The tasks performed by the prospective users may be supported by IS/IT to varying degrees. At this stage, no detailed discussion will be entered into about the IT requirements of any information system, although there will always be a trade-off of cost against functionality.

Various options may be generated, some of which can be rejected before detailed examination in the Investment Appraisal because they fail to meet certain criteria. For example, an option may be rejected because:

- it does not deliver a significant proportion of the benefits already identified as important to the organisation
- it delivers benefits but only in the longer term where immediate payback is required
- it is prohibited on the grounds of cost or risk alone (although detailed costs will not yet be known, clearly high cost or risk options can be identified and discarded). The option delivering the most benefits may be excluded on the basis that it is too costly or represents too high a risk to the business
- it delivers similar benefits to another option, but is clearly more costly or carries a greater risk

- it does not complement, or is not workable with other investments described in the IS strategy – but beware of discarding options that might give a very high return. In such cases it may be sensible to re-examine the strategy.

The number of options which should be selected for detailed Investment Appraisal will vary, but organisations should aim for around three or four. One option *must* be the "do nothing" or "do minimum" option.

5.2 "Do nothing" or baseline option

In business terms, the starting point is to continue operating as at present. This may mean to continue using human resources where there is no IS/IT, or to replace a system which has reached the end of its economic life with something that provides identical functionality and scope at minimum cost and benefits.

This option is fundamental to the appraisal as it will represent the baseline against which costs and benefits will be measured.

It gives to those deciding whether to invest in the information system a clear picture of the present levels of cost benefit and risk which can be compared with other courses of action – for example, investing in IS/IT to enable business change.

The implications of doing nothing must be fully assessed – for example, not meeting targets set in the business plan. Significant resource may be needed to maintain the status quo, for example replacing hardware or maintaining levels of service where volume is increasing.

When defining the baseline, organisations need to measure current performance against which achievement can subsequently be measured. For example, if one of the benefits that the information system should achieve is improved staff morale, organisations must decide the current level of staff morale. In order to do this, organisations will need to give some thought to the measure that they will apply to the benefit, to be refined and validated during the detailed benefits realisation planning described in Chapter 6. In this example, if the measures applied to staff morale are the number of requests for transfer and the number of staff complaints, the baseline should be expressed in this way.

5.3 Scoring options

Choosing the best option may involve scoring each option. The score that each option receives will be driven by the benefits that the organisation wishes to achieve and the importance which the organisation attaches to each of them. The extent to which each option delivers the benefits will determine its score. Different options will deliver the benefits to different degrees and it is at this stage that decisions about how important each generic benefit is and how much of each benefit is to be realised are considered.

Scoring options allows the organisation to rank one option against another (in terms of its global contribution to the organisation) and those scores are meaningful only in relation to each other. So once an option is chosen, the score cannot be used to measure success in achieving benefits.

A number of techniques exist for putting a score on the likely overall benefits that a proposed system delivers to the organisation. A well known approach, *Information Economics* , is described in Annex B and in CCTA's subject guide *Prioritisation*. For the purposes of the benefits optimisation activity, each option can be viewed as a candidate system even though only one will succeed. Whatever technique is used, it is likely to have a number of common features:

- a degree of subjectivity
- use of high level benefit headings to make the scoring manageable
- assignation of ranking and weighting to arrive at a value
- a required high degree of communication, compromise and consensus.

The sophistication of the chosen technique will be dictated by the type of system under examination and the resources available to carry out the exercise, which in turn relate to the importance of the investment. If a consistent basis for decisions and prioritising within the strategy and over time is to be established, organisations should ensure that the same technique is applied to all information systems, such as Cost Benefit Analysis and Discounted Cash Flow.

5.4 Key points for benefits option selection

Key points to consider when deciding which option is selected are that:

- a common understanding of the definitions of each high level benefit exists. A brief written description, with which people agree, of each high level benefit will help to ensure this
- a variety of views are expressed and discussed at the time of decision. People not involved in the decision making process may be inclined to disagree with the chosen option or at the very least will feel no ownership
- there is agreement on the chosen option, or if no agreement can be reached that the key objections against the chosen option are documented
- as far as possible, consistency is obtained in subjective scoring.

Organisations that have undertaken such an exercise strongly favour a workshop approach. Representatives (with authority to make decisions) of all those affected by the decision need to be involved as they will have valid and informed opinions. It may be useful for several workshops (possibly at different levels of seniority within the organisation) to be held to gain the widest selection of views and opinions and to promote ownership of the selected option.

5.5 Who is involved

A number of people will need to be consulted. These include:

- business users who will be affected by, and need to have ownership of the selected business option
- business managers, to help in deciding which is the best option from a business perspective and as those ultimately responsible for realising the benefits
- system developers, who may be in-house or outside suppliers as those responsible for delivering the system will be involved at all stages
- finance divisions.

6 Realising and tracking benefits

When the desired option has been agreed and approved the organisation will know what benefits it expects to obtain. It then needs to make sure that the expected benefits are realised. There should be a policy in place that sets the framework for realising benefits. It will describe how plans for realising benefits will be used. It will also describe the role of reviews to determine whether the planned benefits have been realised; these reviews are described in Chapter 7. This chapter focuses on how an organisation can plan for the realisation of benefits. Figure 12 highlights the stage of realising and tracking benefits.

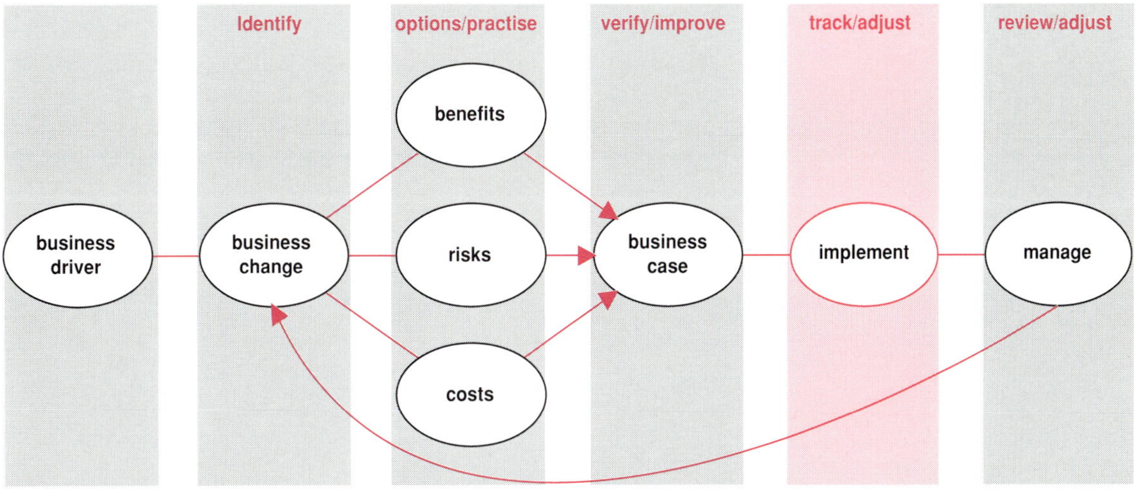

Figure 12 Realising and tracking benefits

There are three major tasks:

- validation of the benefits levels predicted in the business option
- planning the realisation of benefits. This involves producing benefits realisation plans, which will describe how benefits will be measured, and *establishing responsibilities for their achievement*

- tracking the benefits. This requires a tracking regime, which needs to be established and agreed before implementation

6.1 Validating the benefit levels predicted in the business option

The chosen business option will have a predicted level of benefit which the organisation expect to accrue. Detailed technical options would not have been considered at this stage. It may be that during the design stages of the system development certain functionality choices are made in order to reduce costs. It is important to validate the assumptions on which the expected benefit levels were made. It may be necessary to revalidate benefit levels and the Cost Benefit Analysis.

If changes are made – either to the specification, or to the assumptions on which the planned system is based – the benefits must be recalculated. The benefits structure will also need to be checked.

6.2 Planning the realisation of benefits

Benefits realisation plans are essential if the system is to deliver the benefits on which the decision to invest was justified. Responsibility will need to be assigned to individuals. Organisations may wish to be able to aggregate such plans in some way to track overall performance against the business case for the system, or programme where the project forms part of a programme. For example, a system benefits plan might include:

- a definition of the business investment and the objectives
- the name or job title of the sponsor(s)
- a set of benefits with accountabilities and timescales assigned for realisation
- significant benefit dependencies – for example, any high level system or non system requirements which are essential for benefits realisation
- details of the tracking regime to confirm what is to be measured or observed to confirm benefit achievement.

Realisation plans will have a similar structure. *SMART* is a useful mnemonic for defining broadly what a benefits plan should be. It will make them **S**pecific, **M**easurable, **A**chievable, **R**esults oriented and **T**ime oriented. This will involve:

- describing the benefit that is to be realised
- assigning a measure to the benefit
- assigning a target against which achievement will be judged (including a time oriented target)
- documenting the assumptions on which the targets are based
- establishing key responsibilities and authorities for realisation
- establishing a tracking regime/measurement method/collection, responsibilities for tracking, establishing a review framework.

6.3 Describing the benefit to be realised

It is essential to describe the benefit to be realised in direct, simple terms. This will be the basis upon which measurement and responsibilities are assigned and information (and its timing) is collected.

Understanding the benefit in the context of the benefit structure is vital at this stage. For example, it may be that the benefit to be realised initially will be an enabling benefit, a reduction in the number of errors. If this is the case, the organisation would expect this benefit to appear shortly after implementation of the information system, probably at the first PIR conducted 12-18 months following implementation.

6.4 Assigning measures and targets to benefits

Assigning a measure to cash releasing or enhancing benefits is relatively straightforward. *This does not mean that less attention should be paid to them as they will usually form the basis upon which the investment is justified.* Government organisations will have their own well established instructions for measuring this type of benefit. Finance divisions within government organisations will be able to offer advice on the specific rules applying in each organisation.

For quantifiable (but non cash releasing) or not easily quantifiable benefits the process is less simple. No definitive set of measures exists for these types of benefit. However, success in achieving them must be gauged, especially if they have been used in support of cash benefits as a justification for the investment.

The measure will be related directly to the benefit. By quantifying the measure it will become meaningful. For example, if the benefit an organisation is seeking is "increased accuracy", *errors* could be the measurement unit. When this is quantified as the *number* of errors being made, the measure becomes meaningful and can be related to targets. This will be judged against the current state.

Two types of measure that can usefully be applied in the measurement of benefits, are Output and Performance Measure (OPM) and Performance Indicator (PI). The principles that apply to strategy measures also apply to individual systems and there should be a clear linkage between them (individual system or programme benefits must positively contribute to strategy benefits).

It is important to note that:

- OPMs are a direct output measure of results and performance. For example, an OPM for the benefit, "increased customer satisfaction" (in a specific area) would be the number of customers who expressed (a quantified level of) increased satisfaction, compared to the previous level. This would involve interviewing customers regularly and would provide a direct measure of the outcome
- PIs are proxy measures used when performance is not directly measurable or is measurable only at disproportionate cost. Using the above example, if an organisation was not prepared to interview customers on a regular basis, a PI could be applied. This could be the number of complaints (about the specific area) recorded.The organisation would be looking for a reduction.

Organisations will also be aware of the need to have input measures. These will be particularly relevant for measuring economy and effectiveness benefits where input resource for completing an activity (such as staff time) is reduced.

It is important that the OPMs and PIs for *business* benefits are related to *business* performance. Important points for designing OPMs to track benefits are reproduced in Annex C of this guide as a checklist.

6.5 Setting a target

After a measure has been assigned, a target should be assigned against which achievement will be measured. The target will also have a time element which will state when the benefit is expected to be realised. *The target can only be established and will only be relevant when compared with the existing level. This will form the baseline against which performance is measured.*

6.6 Documenting assumptions

The assumptions on which the target benefits have been set should be clearly documented. Although a number of assumptions will have been made explicit in the Investment Appraisal, they should also be clear in the benefits realisation plans. This will allow any under or over achievement of benefits to be assessed before a recommendation for action is made. Documentation is important because under or over achievement may be due to inaccurate assumptions rather than poor management, and this avenue should be explored before readjustment of targets. Examples of assumptions are:

- that the priorities of the organisation remain constant
- required functionality being delivered on time
- external (such as political imperatives) influences remaining unchanged
- successful delivery of training.

The priorities of the organisation must be clearly understood and documented as assumptions, as this will affect the plan's higher order benefits (outcomes). For example, an organisation may plan initially to realise benefits by increasing the quality of service in a number of ways. Severe resource constraints may mean that, at a later stage, this must be sacrificed for economy benefits. The failure to improve customer service is then understood in the context of the business priorities. This particular assumption must be clear so that a change in priorities leads to revised realisation plans, and the collection of information to track them.

6.7 Establishing responsibilities for realisation

Achieving desired outcomes requires management actions and decisions. During the benefits identification activity, a structure of benefits with dependencies will have emerged and organisations will have begun to understand what types of management actions are required to realise them. For example a system can deliver the functionality that saves staff time in carrying out a function, but this itself is not a beneficial outcome. A management action is required to redeploy staff onto other productive duties or to reduce head count.

A decision point must be reached where a benefit enabled by the system is turned into a desired outcome for the organisation. This decision is a business decision, not an IS/IT decision. The way in which authorities are assigned depends on the structure (and culture) of the organisation, but responsibility should be clearly assigned to individuals *who have the authority to realise the benefits and they should sign up to delivery of the benefit*. Generally, the higher up a benefit appears on the benefits structure, the higher the level at which responsibility to achieve the benefit should be assigned.

6.8 The tracking regime

It is important to put in place a tracking regime before implementation, even if the collection of information is not to be carried out until afterwards.This will ensure that the organisation is aware of *what* information needs to be collected, *who* will do it and have responsibility for ensuring it is done, *how* the information will be collected and *when* it needs to be collected. This will assure those responsible for authorising investment in the information system that a mechanism is in place to realise the benefits on which they are agreeing expenditure.

6.9 Collecting information

The information to be collected will be that information which, when analysed, will show the achievement or otherwise of the benefit. It will refer to the measurement units to be applied to the benefit in question. For example if the expected benefit is increased speed of response to customer queries, the measure applied to the benefit could be days elapsed before response. The information required to be collected would then be the number of days elapsed between receipt and response to queries over a specified period.

Who will collect the information

A clear statement of collection duties must be established as part of the tracking regime. These will fall broadly into:

- those who have **responsibility** for ensuring that the information is collected. This will vary according to the organisation. For example it may be the business change manager with responsibility for ensuring that a particular benefit is realised or the IS Executive Committee, if a policy exists within the organisation on benefits tracking
- those who actually collect the information. These may be those people directly employed by the above, as a discrete benefits tracking task. If the information is available in the normal course of the organisation's business (for example, from MIS systems) they may be assigned as extra (marginal) duties. Those employed in the business area where the information system is being implemented (users) may be involved as a necessary part of benefits tracking.

How the information is collected

A description of the way in which the agreed information is collected will refer to the physical collection method. There are a number of methods which will be driven by the way in which the information is generated. The most common are:

- regular data collection. This may be collected on a regular and routine basis as part of the normal working process. Some information may be generated automatically by an information system (either as a core function or a by product), other information may need to be logged (for example, customer satisfaction may require telephone calls of complaint to be logged)
- questionnaires. These will be directed at a pre-determined audience (or a sample), depending on the information sought. They are useful for targeting a large number of people (such as

customers) but response rates are generally low and can vary significantly. Careful consideration should be given to the number of questions, wording etc

- interviews. A precise, but expensive way of obtaining information. Where unexpected benefits accrue the best way of identifying them is to interview users of the information system. Although no baseline is likely to exist to measure them against, they should be recognised and maximised in the future – for example, by exporting good practice.

When the information needs to be collected

It is important to know when information collection has to start and when it has to stop. It may be that where information is expensive to collect (for example, where users have to log activity) a sample over a stated period is sufficient. Although some information may be readily available from existing information systems, it may be convenient to extract that data at certain times rather than as a one- off activity when the data is required for analysis. Where data is not collected continuously, for example where sampling is to be used, care may have to be taken to avoid collection of unrepresentative information – for example, a very busy or slack time of the year. By stating *when* as well as *what* information has to be collected, an organisation will ensure that:

- the information is available when required
- the chances of sub standard or incomplete information being produced is reduced
- resources are better targeted – that is, resource is not wasted by collecting information when it is not required and effort is not expended trying to retrieve information that should have been collected earlier.

Where benefits are high level benefits or outcomes such as improved image, this may take years to fully realise. It may be that (apart from measurements taken to set the baseline), no measurements should be taken for some time.

7 Reviewing and maximising benefits

Reviews take place throughout the business planning cycle and have three objectives relating to IS/IT:

- to assess whether IS/IT is fully contributing to the achievement of business objectives
- to assess whether maximum value for money is obtained from IS/IT in pursuit of the above
- to make recommendations for action.

Although the assessment of benefits realised may be a continuous activity, and does not need to coincide with a formal review, it is at the review stage that specific recommendations and actions are made enable changes to be made to maximise benefits and minimise costs. In this way they may be seen as a broader change and assurance mechanism. Figure 13 highlights the stage of reviewing and maximising benefits.

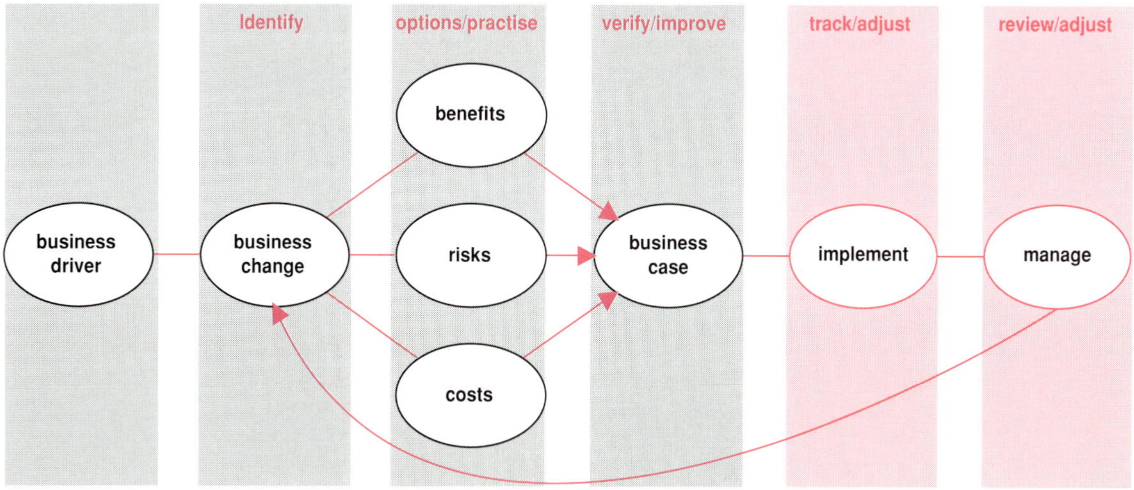

Figure 13 Reviewing and maximising benefits

7.1 The role of formal reviews

Throughout the IS strategy planning process there are various types of review, each with a different purpose. The reviews of particular relevance in managing benefits are those concerned with specific systems – Post Project Evaluations (PPEs). A PPE may be viewed as the sum of a Project Evaluation Review (PER) and Post Implementation Reviews (PIRs). The PER formally concludes the project; later there are reviews to assess how well the system performs against targets (PIR). Throughout the life of a system there will be several PIRs to establish whether the system continues to deliver expected benefits. This chapter focuses mainly on the role of PIRs.

IS strategy review

This is conducted annually, with a major review every three to five years. Briefly, its purpose is to test assumptions on which the strategy was based, review achievements and progress (including the realisation of benefits) and to review business objectives and set targets for the next 12-18 months.

Portfolio review

Organisations will wish to ensure that their portfolio of planned and existing applications (and supporting infrastructure) represents the best way of progressing the IS strategy and achieving business objectives.

Programme review

Where requirements for new systems are identified in the IS portfolio, they will usually be implemented as part of a programme of business change. At the completion of each tranche of a programme there is a specific programme benefit review activity culminating in a programme benefits review report. As part of good programme and project management practice, there will also be reviews during the progression of programmes and individual projects.

PERs

At the conclusion of a project there is a review to establish how well the project was managed in terms of meeting its objectives and delivering within the agreed timescales and resource allocations. This review is *not* concerned with identifying the delivery of benefits.

System PIRs

The benefits management activities described in chapters 3 to 6 of this guide focus on the activities needed before implementation of an information system, to plan successfully the realisation of benefits through effective management. Review of benefits realisation takes place at the PIR stage. It differs from other benefits management activities in that it:

- first takes place after implementation of the information system
- looks back at past achievement, as well as forward
- can act as the catalyst to recommence the benefits management process.

It is important to note that the benefits review activity is only one part of the PIR. Other activities which should be carried out during the PIR to ensure that an individual system fully contributes to business objectives and is delivering maximum value for money in doing so are concerned with cost and risk, but the focus in this guide is on benefits management activities. The benefits review activity of the PIR has three main tasks which are described in this chapter. They are:

- a review of the benefits achieved against those planned and the assumptions on which they were based
- analysing the reasons for under or over achievement, identifying opportunities for further benefits
- making recommendations.

7.2 Timing and frequency of PIRs

Organisation in the private and public sectors are increasingly aware of the need to manage systems throughout their entire lifecycle. Systems will continue to consume resource as long as they exist and if effective use of the IT budget is to be made, this expenditure needs to be set alongside all competing demands for new and existing systems – that is, prioritised. This requires that PIRs are conducted periodically until the end of the information system's life. Each PIR should set the timing for subsequent reviews, which will be governed by the findings and recommendation of the PIR itself – that is, the identified potential for cost, benefit and risk and any action required.

The first PIR will be at least six months after implementation of the system and for large or complex systems, 12-18 months to allow teething problems to be eradicated and for users to become fully familiar with the information system allowing projected benefits to accrue.

But it is important to note that most benefits of strategic importance (such as improved image) may not be realised in full for some years, so a PIR after 12-18 months should be seen as only the first PIR.

7.3 Benefits management and PIRs

The benefits review activity of the benefits management process, carried out during the PIR, will address two major areas; the success in achieving benefits and the success of the benefits management process itself. The following is a suggested minimum checklist of areas that should be addressed:

- which planned benefits have been achieved? If they have been achieved, were the targets correct or should they be increased?
- which planned benefits have not been achieved? Why were the benefits not achieved? Can remedial action be taken to achieve them or must they be foregone?

  Possible reasons for non achievement are:

  - priorities changed, making the realisation of different benefits desirable
  - the benefits claimed were never achievable
  - there was no active management of the benefits to deliver what was achievable
  - some other factor has inhibited achievement
  - benefits were achievable but were not recognised at identification stage
  - changes to requirements and the technical solution during development affected the benefits forecast

- is there any pattern to the success/failure that can be used to inform other realisation plans or further exercises/systems?
- were the assumptions on which the realisation of benefits were based correct? If not what effect did this have on the realisation of benefits?

- were there any unexpected benefits that have resulted? If so can they now be planned and maximised further?
- have identified dis-benefits been managed and minimised? Have the dis-benefits resulted in achievement of benefits of a higher value?
- were there any unexpected dis-benefits that resulted? If so can they now be managed and minimised?
- does the system offer potential for further benefits that warrants a further benefits identification exercise without further investment in IT? (for example, by changing working practices?)
- does the system offer any further potential benefits which would justify further investment in IT?
- do the measures applied to specific benefits appear to be the correct ones? Do they need changing/refining?
- has the collection regime worked?
- re establish the baseline for the next PIR. What are current benefit levels? Do new targets need to be set?
- updating of individual and system benefits plans (which may include realisation plans for higher order benefits expected to come "on stream" before the next PIR).

7.4 Who does the PIRs?

This will be dictated largely by the size of the system and its effects on the organisation. For example, if the effect of the system has been largely to restructure jobs and redeploy staff, business management may feel it necessary to draft in personnel or staff inspection expertise. Generally those conducting PIRs will have, or will draw on expertise from at least:

- IT specialists. Probably drawn from the IS provider to advise on technical risks and the feasibility of any proposed enhancements (but *not* to comment on supplier performance)
- Representatives from the business area. These may be users (although users will definitely be interviewed) or business managers. They will be

able to comment on the support provided for business objectives, business risks, requirements and possible organisational changes

- Finance Division. Organisations may feel it is prudent to have financial (or internal audit) expertise on a PIR team
- Someone who has done PIRs before. This may be internal – for example, management services – or an external consultant (subject to cost constraints).

7.5 Conduct of PIRs

Although it is not possible or desirable to have rigid rules, for the purposes of benefits management the PIR team will use the techniques described at paragraph 6.9. PIRs must be robust enough to identify unexpected benefits and dis-benefits and this will almost certainly involve talking to users of the information system. *They will not be identified purely from examination of documentation.*

Some of the techniques that can be used in conducting a PIR are:

- examination of documentary evidence. Original business case or the last PIR (that is, the baseline), realisation plans, examination of information collected from the data collection regime etc
- if the system is critical to the organisation, interviews with policy sections/top management on any planned large scale business change that may affect the organisation
- interviews with users and customers including internal customers (stakeholders)
- the use of questionnaires to supplement interviews or to replace them where they are not feasible (for example, because of resource constraint) or where specific, structured responses are required
- workshops with business staff to gain insight into current problems and future needs
- assessment of the feasibility of recommendations on other business areas (for example, a recommendation for extra training should be first discussed with the training section)
- sampling techniques.

7.6 Legacy systems

A legacy system may be termed an existing system. It is a system that has been implemented and should form part of the portfolio of applications detailed in the IS strategy. Although they will have different features, a common feature is that they consume resource. While planned systems in the portfolio, identified by the strategic planning process, usually have well defined business objectives, this is often not the case for legacy systems which may have been:

- in existence before the strategic planning discipline was introduced
- the product of an incomplete or poor strategic planning process
- often not properly documented
- in existence before a large scale business or organisational or policy change and have therefore moved away from direct support for business objectives over time
- the product of sound strategic planning, but have not been reviewed for some time since.

The same basic questions need to be addressed for these systems as any other regardless of their original purpose. Do they support business objectives and provide the best value for money in doing so? It will be harder initially to determine this, for a number of reasons:

- the business objectives of the system may no longer be explicit
- the business case for the system may be out of date, or lost
- no benefits baseline may be available
- no current cost baselines may be available. Providers may not have accurate records of current maintenance costs
- the business and technical risks associated with the system may have increased over time but not been recognised or documented
- ownership of the system may have become unclear.

Although the above factors make assessment of the system's contribution (whether positive or negative) to the organisation more difficult, they also make it more imperative. These information systems must therefore be the subject of PIRs. Some organisations, in both the private and public sectors have recognised this need and have developed a programme for the review of legacy systems. If organisations adopt this approach they will wish to consider such factors as:

- the number of legacy systems and the resource that they consume (this may be an approximate figure)
- the pressures on the IS/IT budget
- their perceived importance to the organisation
- the extent to which the IS strategy requires change to achieve its objectives
- the resource available to examine them.

While the process may be more difficult and time consuming – for example, production of a baseline may be required or business objectives may need to be made explicit – the recommendations flowing from them will not differ significantly from others in that they will seek to ensure that the system continues to support business objectives and provides the best value for money in doing so. If a benefits identification activity needs to be carried out, it may be that a system led analysis is the best method.

7.7 Recommending action

If a PIR is to add value, it must do more than track expenditure and performance. It must make recommendations to improve benefits realisation. These may be in the form of remedial action (for example, user training) or to further enhance a system, change working practices etc.

Organisations should guard against the "perpetual project" where enhancements are recommended for very minor business gain. Planned enhancements should be fully prioritised along with other initiatives and the recommendation may be "do nothing". If this is the case, the date for the next PIR would be put back perhaps a year or more. If a number of significant recommendations are made, an early follow up should be recommended.

Depending on the nature of the system, the report should go to the ISSC/ITEC, finance department, business areas affected and other relevant sections.

PIRs provide valuable information that should feed back to the IS strategy planning process and inform the way in which the strategy is developed in future. Lessons learned in this way facilitate the process of achieving benefits from investment in information systems.

Annexes

A Examples of benefits

Potential benefits	Most likely investment appraisal category		
	Direct financial benefits	*Direct non-financial benefits*	*Indirect benefits*
Staff savings	•		
Work downgraded	•		
Overtime reduced	•		
Travelling time and cost reduced	•		
Consumables reduced	•		
Less accommodation required	•		
Manning for peaks avoided	•		
Greater accuracy		•	
Tasks eliminated	•		
New tasks taken on	•		
More work taken on	•		
Better forecasts		•	
Better image			•
More reliable information		•	
More creative thinking time			•
Improved turnround time		•	
Quicker production time		•	
Better quality output		•	
Improved presentation		•	
Lower staff turnover		•	
Better attendance	•		
More job satisfaction			
More flexible working		•	
Better tools/facilities/services		•	
Hands-on experience			
Smoother peaks/troughs	•		
Better management control		•	
Wider spans of control	•		
Easier communications		•	
Greater organisational flexibility		•	
Lesson learning		•	
Flexibility of approach to calls for change or new tasks		•	

B Information Economics

Information Economics

The basis of the Information Economics approach is to assign a weighting to the importance of each generic benefit for the organisation and to assign a score, specific to the option under consideration which rates the extent to which the option satisfies that particular generic benefit. Thus, the weighting is constant across the exercise and the ratings vary according to the option under consideration. Multiplication of the weights by the ratings will give each application a score for each generic benefit. By adding together the scores for each benefit a preferred (benefit) option will be reached. In summary, the steps for using the Information Economics approach are:

a allocate a weighting to the most important generic benefit heading. Rate this with a weight of, for example 10 or 100

b examine the other generic benefit headings in a "pairwise" comparison. This consists of selecting the other generic benefit headings and deciding how much less important each is than the most important one and in relation to each other and weighting them accordingly

c examine each option in turn against each of the generic benefit headings. Briefly describe how that option meets the generic benefit headings, without scoring

d score each of the options against each of the generic benefit headings. The better an option performs, the higher the score against each generic benefit heading.

By weighting the generic benefits, the organisation will be making broad decision about how the benefits are to be realised (that is, the mix of benefits). For example, if the generic benefit heading, economy is given a high weighting, this will imply that (at this time) the organisation intends to realise much of the benefits as cash releasing benefits (for example by reducing head count). *The way in which benefits are realised will be driven by the needs and priorities for the business at the time.*

C OPMs to track the realisation of benefits

There are a number of important points to consider when designing OPMs to track the realisation of benefits. It is important to consider:

- OPMs already available from other sources, such as statistics collection, or policy evaluation
- when benefits are planned to accrue. Are they likely to occur continuously, as regular events, or once only? If once, at some distant point, what can be monitored as evidence of progress towards the final event (for example, intermediate objectives or related milestones)?
- the objectives that the benefit producing information system is supporting - are there OPMs attached to it? If so, can they be used?
- the CSFs associated with the realisation of benefits - that is, what is crucial to their successful realisation
- setting realistic targets - trends of previous, related outputs might provide a guide
- the cost of collecting OPM values - where this seems extreme, consider alternative OPMs
- whether the aggregation of OPMs is desirable at some stage, for example for presentation to senior management.

Further reading

CCTA publications	The following CCTA publications provide further information on topics covered in this guide:
Investment appraisal	IS Guide B4: *Appraising Investment in Information Systems* – ISBN 0-471-925225, John Wiley and Sons Ltd (1989)
	IS Planning Guide *Appraisal and Evaluation of IS Strategies*, CCTA (1991)
Managing IS/IT	IS Guide A2 *Strategic Planning for Information Systems* – ISBN 0-471-925225, John Wiley and Sons Ltd (1989)
	Managing IS/IT for the Business – the Role of the Intelligent Customer CCTA 1994
Policies	IS Planning Guide *Policies and IS Strategies*, HMSO (1993)
Programme management	*An Introduction to Programme Management* – ISBN 0 11 330611 3, HMSO (1993)
	Guide to Programme Management – ISBN 0 11 330600 8, HMSO (1994).
Other publications	*Economic Appraisal in Central Government: A Technical Guide for Government Departments (The Green Book)*, HM Treasury, April 1991; available from HMSO.

Glossary

business benefits	The financial and non-financial benefits that will accrue to the organisation through the implementation of information systems and the supporting infrastructure.
business case	The purpose of the business case is to provide an overall justification for the proposals; the basis of comparison is the Base Case.
business objectives	The measurable milestones that mark progress towards achieving the organisation's aims.
economy	Obtaining the same goods or services more cheaply. The comparison may be made between suppliers, say, or over time. It is usually expressed in terms of savings.
effectiveness	The extent to which objectives have been achieved, expressed as the ratio of actual output to planned output. For example, if it were planned to process 100 applications and 80 were done, effectiveness would be 80%.
efficiency	A comparison of output with the input required to produce it. For example, if 16 mandays were taken to process 80 applications, efficiency would be 5 applications per manday. Unit cost is a measure of how much it costs to produce one unit of output and is another way of expressing efficiency – for example, the unit cost of processing applications is £8.50.
information systems (IS)	Any procedure or process, with or without IT support, which provides a way of acquiring, storing, processing, or disseminating information. Information systems include applications and their supporting infrastructure components.
information technology (IT)	The use of micro-electronics-based combination of computing and telecommunications to provide information systems.

infrastructure
Refers to both IT infrastructure (the hardware, software, and computer-related communications that support the ongoing provision of the IT service) and/or organisational infrastructure (management, organisation, finance). Infrastructure systems are a sub-set of information systems.

investment appraisal
A technique used to identify the costs and benefits attributable to alternative of meeting objectives and requiring the use of discounted cash flow (DCF) in presenting the results.

IS strategy
A formal definition of the intended future deployment of IS, and its supporting policies, programmes of work and infrastructure within a department in support of business objectives.

option appraisal
The process by which the various ways of meeting business needs are evaluated against a set of selection criteria, including economic appraisal, and the option representing best value for money is selected.

performance measurement
A means of establishing how well a service is performing by comparing actual performance with planned targets.

Post Implementation Review (PIR)
A formal mechanism to determine the extent to which a completed project has met its objectives and realised the expected benefits.

programme management
The selection and co-ordinated planning of a portfolio of projects so as to achieve a set of defined business objectives and the efficient execution of these projects, within a controlled environment, such that they realise maximum benefit for the resulting business operations.

value for money (VFM)
Value for money comes from the effective, efficient and economic use of resources. It is a balance of quality, time, cost and risk. Value is a relative property in terms of relevance to the requirement, and in relation to available alternatives for spending the money. Value for money therefore depends on the decisions and choices made, as well as the eventual realisation of operational systems.

Printed in England for HMSO
Dd 300157 12/94 C10 3400/3